Eco Alert!
SAVING WILDLIFE

Rebecca Hunter

SEA-TO-SEA

Mankato Collingwood London

This edition first published in 2012 by

Sea-to-Sea Publications
Distributed by Black Rabbit Books
P.O. Box 3263, Mankato, Minnesota 56002

9 8 7 6 5 4 3 2

Published by arrangement with the Watts
Publishing Group Ltd, London.

Library of Congress Cataloging-in-Publication Data

Hunter, Rebecca, 1935-
  Saving wildlife / by Rebecca Hunter.
      p. cm. -- (Eco alert)
  Includes index.
  ISBN 978-1-59771-298-9 (library binding)
  1. Wildlife conservation--Juvenile literature. I. Title.
  QL83.H86 2012
  333.95'416--dc22

                          2011001202

Planning and production by
Discovery Books Limited
Managing Editor: Rachel Tisdale
Editor: Rebecca Hunter
Designer: Blink Media
Picture Research: Rebecca Hunter

February 2011
RD/6000006415/001

Photographs: **Corbis:** page 22 (Alex Hoffard/EPA),
page 28 (Jon Hrusa/EPA); **Gardener's World/BBC:**
page 29 top; **Getty Images:** page 5 bottom right
(AFP), page 5 bottom left (Daniel Delgado), page 8
(AFP), page 9 bottom (China Photos), page 10
(Gallo Images), page 21 (Photolibrary), page 26
(Bates Littlehales), page 27 (Visuals Unlimited);
Greenpeace: page 7 (Paul Hilton); **Istock:** page 13
(Richard Carey), page 15 (Fenghui), page 19
(Interbober), page 20 (dino4), page 23
(photoGartner), page 29 bottom (JurgaR); **Lewa
Wildlife Conservancy:** page 11; **Science Photo
Library:** page 13 inset (R Van Nostrand), page 18
(Tom Mchugh); **Shutterstock:** Cover (Kristian
Sekulic), page 4 (Jason Vandehey), page 6 (Mark
R), page 9 top (Stephen Meese), page 12 (Kavram),
page 14 (Artconcept), page 16 (Szefei), page 17
(Eric Gevaert), page 24 (Bonnie Fink), page 25
(David Aleksandrowicz).

Every attempt has been made to clear copyright.
Should there be any inadvertent omission please
apply to the publisher for rectification.

Contents

4 The Sixth Extinction

6 Overhunting of Animals

8 Poaching

10 Saving the Rhino

12 Habitat Loss

14 Fragmentation

16 Orangutans at Risk

18 Competition and Predation

20 Flightless Birds

22 Pollution and Disease

24 Climate Change

26 Captive Breeding

28 The Future of Wildlife

30 Glossary

31 Further Information

32 Index

The Sixth Extinction

Did you know that most of the **species** that have ever lived on Earth are now **extinct**? Did you know that the majority of life on Earth has never been known to us? Every day many species of animals, perhaps hundreds, become extinct without us even knowing they existed.

Throughout the Earth's history species have become extinct due to natural causes. Scientists recognize that there have been five mass extinctions caused by **astronomical**, **geological**, or **volcanic** events. Each of these extinctions wiped out between 50 and 95 percent of the wildlife of the time. The most recent of these was about 65 million years ago, when a giant asteroid is thought to have collided with the Earth. This brought about the extinction of three quarters of the Earth's animal species including the dinosaurs. After a mass extinction like this, it takes at least 10 million years for the **biological diversity** to recover.

⊙ Ammonites were marine mollusks that lived hundreds of millions of years ago. They became extinct at the same time as the dinosaurs, about 65 million years ago. Their fossilized remains are found throughout the world.

Today we are living in the middle of a sixth great extinction. Unlike the others, this one has a different cause—human activity. It probably began 50,000 years ago when early humans started to migrate around the world and began hunting with Stone Age weapons.

Since the 1600s, more than 250 large animal species became extinct—every one caused by humans. Over 16,000 more are threatened with extinction. This loss is due to the damage and pollution of the environment, loss of habitats, overhunting, agriculture, and the introduction of alien species.

Once an animal species is extinct, it is gone forever. We need to act now to conserve the amazing biodiversity on our planet and to ensure it will be there for future generations.

HOT SPOT:

Last One Left!

George the tortoise (below) is the very last of a species of Galapagos island giant tortoise. He lives on the island of Pinta and has been in captivity for 36 years. He is literally the rarest animal in the world!

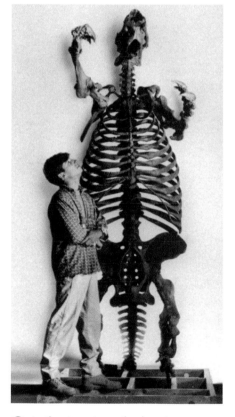

◉ In the Americas, the hunting activities of early humans eventually caused a continent-wide extinction of animals such as saber-toothed cats, wild horses, and ground sloths—a fossilized skeleton of which is seen here.

Overhunting of Animals

Ever since early people learned how to make weapons, humans have hunted animals for their **hides**, meat, and bones. They often had no knowledge of what damage they were doing to the animal populations and hunted many to extinction.

Already Extinct

The passenger pigeon was once probably the most numerous bird on the planet. It lived in North America and flew in flocks so large that they darkened the sky for hours and sometimes days as they passed overhead. It was driven to extinction by uncontrolled hunting by early European settlers in the 1800s. A species that once numbered more than four billion individuals was gone in a few decades.

American Bison

The American bison was almost hunted to extinction in the nineteenth century by Native American people and European settlers who wanted their meat and hides. Bison hunting was big business and whole herds were killed daily. One professional hunter alone killed more than 20,000 animals. Eventually, as the great herds disappeared, plans were made to save the bison. From a small number of privately owned herds, the bison population began to recover and now they are no longer endangered.

How can you help?

Buy fish that come from marine stocks that aren't being overfished. If you eat tuna, only buy line-caught, skipjack tuna.

⊙ Approximately 3,500 bison live in Yellowstone National Park today. These animals are descendents of the small population of 23 bison that survived the mass slaughter of the 1800s.

Whale Hunting

Whales have been heavily hunted for many years for their meat, **blubber**, **baleen,** and whale oil. Now many species are endangered and face extinction. Conservation methods include setting hunting quotas, declaring the Indian Ocean a whale sanctuary, and protecting the seven most endangered species. But whales reproduce slowly. For example, the right whale has been protected for more than 50 years and still numbers less than 400 animals.

⊕ Fishing for tuna is done on an industrial scale. Some tuna ships take 3,000 tons of fish out of the sea in a single trip. Here a Greenpeace boat makes a protest against the *Albatuna Tres,* the world's largest tuna fishing vessel.

Animal Status	
Today overhunting is pushing many animals to the brink of extinction. The International Union for Conservation of Nature has a scale that shows the status of animals in the wild.	
Extinct	none of the species is left at all
Extinct in the wild	none of the species survive in the wild but some exist in captivity
Critically endangered	the species faces a high risk of being extinct very soon
Endangered	the species is in danger of becoming extinct
Vulnerable	not yet classified as endangered but numbers are dropping
Near threatened	species numbers may be dropping
Least concern	species numbers are stable

Poaching

Poaching is the illegal hunting, killing, or capturing of animals. Some animals are poached for food, but many more are taken for their hides and furs, and for medicines and trophies.

Cruel Methods

Poachers have no interest in animal welfare and often kill animals in cruel ways. Animals caught in traps and snares suffer badly before the trapper arrives to kill them. Poisoning is another method that poachers use, which causes animals to die in terrible pain. Some animals are captured live for the pet trade. People want exotic baby animals as pets and poachers can kill whole family groups in order to get just a few youngsters.

Elephant Poaching

African elephants once roamed the entire African continent but now inhabit less than one third of it. Poachers kill elephants for their ivory tusks, which are wanted in countries such as China and India. Whole herds of elephants can be killed just to get the tusks from a few adults. There has been a ban on the international ivory trade since the 1980s, which has allowed some populations of elephants to reestablish. However, recent investigations show that ivory poaching is increasing. In 2009 customs officials in Vietnam seized sections of tusks from up to 900 elephants. Poaching levels are thought to be putting the remaining wild elephant population in danger of extinction.

⊙ A keeper feeds a baby elephant at the Nairobi Elephant Nursery in Kenya. The nursery rears elephants that have been orphaned by poaching. The recent rise in poaching has led to more elephant babies being rescued by the orphanage.

HOT SPOT:

The Amur Leopard

With fewer than 35 left in the wild, the Amur leopard (above) is considered the world's most endangered cat. It has been hunted for its skin and is now in immediate danger of extinction. **Conservationists** are trying hard to save it, but it may be too late.

Wild Tigers

The number of tigers in the wild is rapidly declining. They are killed for their skins and also to supply bones and body parts for traditional Chinese medicine. There are thought to be more tigers in captivity now than there are in the wild. A recent survey of the Bengal tiger showed there are fewer than 1,400 left in India—half the number there were in 2002.

◄ An illegal collection of tiger, leopard, and otter skins is inspected by a customs official in China. The skins will now be given to the Chinese Academy of Sciences for use in research and education.

How can you help?

Adopt a tiger through the WWF. Your money will go toward saving tiger habitats and protecting them from illegal poachers. See page 31 for web site details.

Saving the Rhino

There are five species of rhinoceros, two in Africa and three in southern Asia. All of them have been persistently hunted for their horns, which are used in traditional Asian medicine and also as dagger handles in the Middle East.

The Black Rhino

The population of the black rhino is steadily declining. From at least 100,000 animals in 1960, there are thought to be fewer than 4,500 left today. Most of these survive in countries where there are good antipoaching programs, such as South Africa, Kenya, Namibia, and Zimbabwe.

Conservation Measures

Many measures have been taken to save the rhino. The animals have been protected since 1976 by CITES (Convention on International Trade in Endangered Species, see page 28), which aims to stop the trade in rhino parts. Many rhinos were moved to fenced and guarded **sanctuaries** in the early 1990s, which has increased populations in some areas.

HOT SPOT:

Lewa Wildlife Conservancy

The Lewa Wildlife Conservancy has helped save the black rhino in Kenya. The 62,000-acre (25,000-ha) reserve is surrounded by an electric fence, which guards patrol daily. Lewa now has 67 black rhinos. The sanctuary is very proud that it has never lost a rhino to poachers.

▶ A ranger in KwaZulu Natal, South Africa, shows a collection of rhino horns that has been **confiscated** from poachers.

10

In Zimbabwe an attempt was made to stop poaching by dehorning rhinos in the National Parks. Unfortunately the plan did not work. More than 80 dehorned rhinos were killed by poachers in one year alone.

The White Rhino

The white rhino is an example of an animal that has made an amazing comeback from the brink of extinction. About 100 years ago, barely 20 rhinos were left in the KwaZulu Natal province in South Africa. The area became a rhino sanctuary and the number of animals grew to such an extent that it was able to provide **stock** to reintroduction programs all over Africa. There are now thought to be about 14,500 white rhinos living in Africa.

How can you help?

Tusk Trust supports the Lewa Conservancy and many other projects across Africa dedicated to protecting wildlife. Visit their web site and see how your could help save the rhino and other endangered species. (See page 31 for website details.)

⊙ A pair of white rhinos with a game ranger in a reserve in Kenya. Thanks to dedicated teams of rangers like this one, the white rhino is no longer in danger of extinction.

Habitat Loss

A habitat is the natural home of an animal. Animals adapt to live in a particular type of habitat. Some need tall trees to live in and breed; others may need fresh running water. When an animal's habitat is damaged or destroyed, it usually cannot survive.

Vanishing Wetlands

Swamps and **salt marshes** are being drained all over the world to make more space for agricultural fields. Many species of frogs and other amphibians are threatened by this habitat loss. It is thought that most of the 4,500 species of frogs are expected to become extinct within decades.

Deforestation

Forests are one of the most threatened of all habitats. They are cut down to provide land for farming and to supply wood for the **timber** industry. More than half of the world's forests have been cut down already and the rate of **deforestation** is increasing. The tropical **rain forests** contain the largest **biodiversity** of wildlife on the planet and many species living in this habitat are becoming endangered or are already extinct.

⊙ Agriculture is one of the worst destroyers of habitats. Many types of habitat were destroyed when these fields in Montana were created. This will have led to a huge loss in local biodiversity.

HOT SPOT:

Northern Hairy-Nosed Wombat

The Australian northern hairy-nosed wombat is classified as critically endangered and is one of the rarest animals in the world. Its scrub habitat has been taken over by cattle ranchers and the native grasses it likes to feed on are being replaced by other plants.

Ocean Habitats in Danger

In the last 50 years habitat destruction has spread to the seas. Fishing by "dragging," a method where a metal chain scrapes across the seabed, is hugely destructive to the animals and plants that live there. Dragging is thought to have endangered about two-thirds of the world's fish stocks.

Six of the seven species of marine turtle are listed as endangered or critically endangered. Development of coastlines with hotels and other buildings has destroyed many of their nesting beaches. When young turtles do hatch, lights from roads and buildings often distract them away from the sea and into danger.

The hawksbill turtle is a critically endangered sea turtle found throughout the world's oceans. It is illegal to catch or sell hawksbill turtles or their shells.

Coral reefs are threatened by fishing, sedimentation, and global warming.

Fragmentation

Fragmentation is a form of habitat loss that happens when an animal's habitat is broken up into smaller pieces by roads, settlements, or other obstacles. It prevents animals from moving around freely and makes it difficult for them to find food, shelter, or mates.

Genetic Inbreeding

One of the results of fragmentation is that animal populations become smaller. Small populations are likely to suffer from **inbreeding**. Because there are fewer choices of mate, animals are forced to breed with close relatives. The general health of the population declines. The animals are more likely to catch diseases and are less adaptable to changes in the environment.

Wildlife Crossings

The building of roads, railroads, and walls can create major barriers to animals, because there is no way they can cross them. One possible solution is to construct wildlife crossings through which the animals can move. These can be overpasses for large animals, or tunnels for small mammals and amphibians.

HOT SPOT:

Tunnels in the Netherlands

More than 600 tunnels have been installed so that animals can go under roads in the Netherlands. This has noticeably helped the population levels of the endangered European badger.

▶ The monarch butterfly is becoming threatened in the central U.S. as its **prairie** home becomes fragmented by huge grain farms. The butterfly only survives in small islands of undisturbed habitat between fields.

14

The Giant Panda

The world's favorite endangered animal, the giant panda, is suffering from loss of habitat due to fragmentation. Economic development in China means there is more demand for **infrastructure** such as roads, railroads, and mines. These cut directly through panda habitats. Many panda populations are left living in isolated "island" spots. The pandas are unable to migrate, so their habitats become overcrowded. Some small populations are expected to die out within a few generations.

⊙ The giant panda reserve at Wolong, China, is the world's largest breeding center for pandas and is home to 142 captive pandas. It was badly damaged in an earthquake in 2008, but there are plans to rebuild an even larger center.

Orangutans at Risk

Orangutans are the only big apes found in Asia. They live on the islands of Borneo and Sumatra, and are at risk because their rain forest habitat is being cut down to plant oil palm trees.

The Palm Oil Explosion

Palm oil is used mainly in cooking, but also in cosmetics and biofuel. It is a very profitable crop and is exported all over the world. In Indonesia there are already 15 million acres (six million hectares) of oil palm plantations but huge areas of rain forest are cleared every day to plant more. It is thought that the orangutan may lose its tropical home within 15 years.

When their rain forest habitat is destroyed, orangutans have to search further for food. Many orangutans are shot by farmers when they raid oil-palm plantations.

⊙ An oil palm plantation in Sumatra. The Indonesian government plans to put huge areas of land into palm-oil production by 2015.

The Pet Trade

Orangutan babies look very cute and people will pay a high price to buy one as a pet. Despite it being illegal to own an orangutan, poachers kill mothers so that their babies can be shipped abroad for the pet trade. Many die on the journey. It is thought that about 5,000 animals will die to get just 1,000 babies. Those that become pets may only live for a few years. Once they grow up, they become unmanageable and most will end up being put to sleep.

Saving Orangutans

The Borneo Orangutan Survival Foundation is the largest primate-rescue project in the world. The project rescues wild orangutans from oil palm plantations as well as looking after hundreds of orphaned orangutan infants. Each baby has its own human caretaker who looks after it night and day.

How can you help?

Some of the timber that is cut down in rain forests can be used to make souvenirs for tourists. If you are on vacation, make sure you don't buy goods that come from this source. Try to buy things that come from a sustainable source.

⊙ A baby orangutan with its mother. Young orangutans spend about six years with their mothers before they are old enough to survive on their own. Rearing them in captivity is a long and dedicated job.

Competition and Predation

When humans introduce a new species into a region either on purpose or by mistake, the original species that lived there will often suffer. Either they are preyed upon by the new animal or they cannot compete with it for food.

Island Communities

Competition and predation from introduced species can be seen most clearly on islands. Island ecosystems evolved in isolation from other populations and their inhabitants often have no natural predators.

When Columbus first sailed to America in the late fifteenth century, his ships accidentally brought over the black rat. When he landed on the islands of the West Indies, these rats swam ashore and multiplied. The West Indian island shrews could not compete with the rats and were wiped out by the early 1500s.

Extinctions in Australia

Four frogs, 23 birds, and 27 mammal species are known to have become extinct since European settlers arrived in Australia. Their deaths were caused by the introduction of three species; the European rabbit, the red fox, and the domestic cat. Many animals continue to be threatened today and Australia has more endangered species than any other continent.

⊙ The brush-tailed rat-kangaroo is a small marsupial found in Australia. It once ranged over 60 percent of the Australian mainland, but today inhabits less than 1 percent, mainly because of competition from introduced grazing animals.

Hedgehogs in the Hebrides

In 1974, a few hedgehogs were introduced to a Scottish island to control slugs and snails in an islander's garden. They multiplied quickly and spread to three islands. Their numbers reached more than 5,000 and they started having a devastating impact on populations of ground-nesting wading birds. Plans to cull the hedgehogs were stopped by animal welfare groups and now the animals are being captured and relocated to the mainland.

⊙ The Australian possum was introduced into New Zealand in the 1800s. Its numbers have increased enormously and it is now a danger to both the vegetation and the native birdlife.

Introduced Possums

Possums were introduced into New Zealand by the government to start a trade in fur. At the height of the fur trade, trappers killed over 20 million possums in a year. After the loss of the fur trade in the 1990s, possum numbers increased dramatically. Possums have no natural **predators** in New Zealand and there are now more than 30 million in the country. They are causing huge damage to the natural forests and compete with birds for food. Sometimes they eat their eggs and chicks as well. In the 1970s, there were 140 bird species in the South Island. Now there are only 29.

Flightless Birds

On remote islands where there are no natural predators, many birds have lost the need to fly. Unfortunately when predatory species, including humans, are introduced they have no means of escape.

Hunted by Humans

The moa was once the tallest bird on Earth, standing more than 13 feet (4 m) tall. Despite its size, the moa had no means of escape or defense and it was hunted to extinction immediately after the first human settlement of New Zealand in the thirteenth century.

The dodo was a flightless bird that lived on the island of Mauritius in the Indian Ocean. Like many animals that evolved in isolation from predators, the dodo was totally unafraid of people, so it was easy prey for Dutch sailors in the mid-seventeenth century. The dogs, pigs, cats, and rats the Dutch brought with them also probably contributed to its final extinction in about 1680.

▶ The dodo became extinct just 100 years after it was first discovered by Dutch sailors on the island of Mauritius.

New Zealand's Endangered Birds

During New Zealand's millions of years of isolation, many birds developed various levels of flightlessness together with ground-feeding and nesting habits. As a result these birds were at great risk when human settlement started 700 years ago. More than 42 percent of its bird species have now been lost; 57 birds have become extinct; and nine are now critically endangered. The introduction of species such as stoats and ferrets has endangered many of these species. It is estimated that stoats kill 15,000 brown kiwi chicks a year in the North Island and the kiwi population is halving every decade.

⊙ The kakapo, the world's largest parrot, is being brought back from the brink of extinction by a breeding program on Codfish Island off the south coast of New Zealand. In 2009, 24 chicks were hatched, bringing the population up to 124 birds. It is hoped that the birds will one day be reintroduced to the mainland.

Pollution and Disease

Pollution from agriculture and industry causes many problems for wildlife, while small populations suffer great threats from disease.

Acid Rain

Chemicals released into the air by factories and some power stations can combine with water to produce rain that is acidic. When this falls, it kills trees and pollutes water. In the Adirondack Mountains in New York State, the hundreds of lakes and ponds that were once filled with trout, frogs, and salamanders are now clear and empty of any life. In some areas, lakes are being sprayed with lime to try to correct the acidity of the water.

The Yangtze River Dolphin

The Yangtze River dolphin, which has lived in China's Yangtze River for the last 20 million years, has now been declared extinct. Recent expeditions have failed to find a single animal. The last known dolphin died in captivity in 2002.

⊙ The Yangtze River dolphin is now extinct. The dolphin was threatened by shipping traffic, overfishing, and general pollution of the river, which is one of the most polluted in the world.

Threatened by Disease

The European red squirrel has been declining in numbers for many years due to habitat loss and competition with the gray squirrel, introduced from the United States. It is now suffering from a new threat, a virus that kills it within weeks. The disease is spread by gray squirrels but does not affect them. Scientists are trying to find a **vaccine** to protect the red squirrel.

◀ Britain's red squirrel, now one of the UK's most endangered animals.

Bees in Danger

Honeybees around the world are declining due to the spread of a parasite called the Varroa mite. This is a serious problem for farmers because bees pollinate around 60 percent of all food produced. The mite is resistant to chemicals, so researchers are trying to find other ways of getting rid of it.

How can you help?

Grow as many types of flower in your yard as possible to encourage bees and other pollinating insects. Bees like colorful flowers such as sunflowers, poppies, and lupins.

Climate Change

The climate of Earth has changed enormously over its history. Many animals in the past could not adapt to the changes and died out. Forty-thousand years ago in Australia, a series of massive droughts wiped out many large animal species such as giant kangaroos, enormous wombats, and massive emus. Our current trend of global warming may lead to the loss of more animal species.

Mammals in Danger

The American pika, a small relative of the rabbit, lives in high, rocky areas and needs a cool, moist climate. As temperatures rise, the pikas have to climb higher every year. There will soon be nowhere else for them to go and already many populations are dying out every summer.

The first mammal believed to have become extinct due to recent global warming is the white possum. This animal, native to Australia, has not been seen in nearly four years. Record temperatures in 2005 may have caused its extinction. Only five hours of temperatures above 86°F (30°C) will kill the possum.

⊙ American pikas cannot easily migrate in response to climate change because their habitats are restricted to small, fragmented "islands" at the top of mountain ranges.

Declining Amphibians

Amphibians are more susceptible to climate change than other types of animal. Because of their **permeable** skin, unshelled eggs, and dependence on water, they are extremely sensitive to small changes in temperature and moisture. Many amphibian populations are known to be declining worldwide and the golden toad of Costa Rica is already extinct.

Coral Reefs Dissolving

Scientists believe that the amount of carbon dioxide in the atmosphere has passed the safe level for the world's coral reefs. The Great Barrier Reef off the east coast of Australia has been affected by warmer temperatures, which kill the **algae** on which the coral depend, and increased acidity, which dissolves the coral's **exoskeleton**. It is possible that the world's coral reefs are in danger of disappearing completely in the next 20 years.

⊙ More than one million species of fish and **invertebrates** make their homes and feed among coral reefs. It will be a tragedy if this wonderfully diverse ecosystem is destroyed because of climate change.

Captive Breeding

One way in which an endangered animal species can be saved is to breed it in captivity. If the numbers of the species are increased significantly, it is sometimes possible to reintroduce it to the wild.

Père David's Deer

Captive breeding has proved successful with several critically endangered species, the earliest example being the Père David's deer. The Père David's deer is a Chinese deer that was extinct in the wild by the nineteenth century. The only animals remaining were 18 individuals in Europe that were collected together at the Duke of Bedford's estate at Woburn Abbey, in England. The animals bred well and eventually they were reintroduced to two sites in China. Now they number more than 1,300 in the wild with many more in captivity. The species was probably the first to be saved from extinction.

⊙ A herd of Père David's deer graze in the grounds of Woburn Abbey, in England. The species was saved from extinction at this mansion.

Saving the Californian Condor

Californian condors are one of the most endangered birds in the world. In 1987, only 22 of them remained. These were captured and a breeding program begun. The eggs were removed as they were laid, to encourage the female to lay more. The eggs were **incubated** and the chicks raised by hand. As a result of captive breeding, the condor population had increased to more than 320 birds by 2009.

◀ The North American black-footed ferret is one of the most endangered mammals in the world. At one point, there were fewer than 20 individuals left in the wild. A successful captive-breeding program has bred more than 6,500 ferrets since 1987.

HOT SPOT:

The Black Robin

The black robin is found only on the Chatham Islands in the South Pacific, and was once the world's rarest bird. In 1980, there were just one female bird and four males left. A program was started, which involved actively removing the female's eggs and giving them to other birds to hatch. This encouraged the female to lay more eggs. The fostering program has been so successful that there are now about 250 black robins on the islands.

Problems with Captive Breeding

One of the problems of captive breeding is telling whether the animal will survive when it is released back into the wild. Many animals lose their survival skills after years in captivity. They may have to be taught how to find food, avoid predators, attract a mate, and find shelter. Another problem is inbreeding. Breeders try hard to prevent this, but most captive populations are based on a very small number of individuals. Unwanted characteristics can become common. For example, in a fish-breeding program a population of **albino** trout appeared. In the wild, an albino fish would be preyed upon quickly and the **trait** would not be passed on to the next generation.

The Future of Wildlife

Many animals are threatened today as a result of human actions. We have a duty to preserve and protect the species on our planet. In some cases, such as the bee, we cannot survive without them. Fortunately there are many ways in which we can help save wildlife.

Convention on International Trade in Endangered Species

One protection method is to try to halt the trade in endangered species. More than 160 countries have signed the Convention on International Trade in Endangered Species (CITES). This protects more than 5,000 animal and 28,000 plant species. CITES works by controlling the import and export of these species. Trade in species threatened with extinction is banned, while trade in other endangered species requires special licenses.

An official walks through a warehouse containing stockpiled ivory in the Kruger National Park, South Africa. This ivory will be sold to buyers in China and Japan in a deal approved by CITES. The ivory was obtained from natural deaths and culling, and the profits made from their sale will go back into elephant conservation programs.

LOT 11
WEIGHT: 1385.90 kg

South African
NATIONAL PARKS

Protected Areas

Protecting habitats by making wildlife parks and reserves can help wild animals live and breed safely. In 1975, the Great Barrier Reef was declared a marine park. The Great Barrier Reef is the world's largest collection of coral and is still at risk despite being protected. Fishing and the removal of coral or shells is strictly regulated and shipping traffic must follow defined routes that avoid the most sensitive areas of coral.

Making Wildlife Pay

One way to ensure that people conserve the wildlife in their area is by making wildlife profitable. **Ecotourism** has become a big earner in many parts of the world and in some cases, former poachers have turned into tour guides. In Uganda, groups of tourists are taken to interact with mountain gorillas, while in southern Africa, tourists gather to watch elephants and rhino. Ecotourism is rapidly becoming a good way for developing countries to bring in money.

How can you help?

Build a wildlife stack in your yard out of pipes, sticks, plant pots, and tiles, to provide shelter for amphibians, ladybugs, and other insects.

⊙ Whale watching has become popular in many places from North America to New Zealand.

Glossary

Albino
A loss of pigment that causes animals to appear pale or white with pink eyes.

Algae
A type of plant that grows in water but does not have true leaves, roots, or stems.

Astronomical
Relating to things in space.

Baleen
A special type of bone found in whales.

Biodiversity
The range of living things present in an area.

Biological diversity
The quantity and variety of plant and animal species living in a place.

Blubber
The fat from a whale.

Confiscate
To remove property legally from somebody.

Conservationists
People who try to save wildlife and the environment.

Deforestation
The cutting down of forests.

Ecotourism
Tourists paying to see wildlife in its natural habitat without disturbing it.

Exoskeleton
The external skeleton of an animal, for example, a tortoise's shell.

Extinct
Describes species of animal that have no living members left.

Fragmentation
The dividing up of a habitat by roads, railroads, and other man-made structures.

Geological
Relating to the natural forces on Earth.

Hides
The skins of large animals.

Inbreeding
Breeding with close relations over many generations.

Incubate
To keep eggs warm so that the animal inside can grow and hatch out.

Infrastructure
The basic physical and organizational structures needed for a human society to exist in a place.

Invertebrates
Small animals without backbones such as worms, insects, and spiders.

Permeable
Allowing liquids or gases to pass through.

Prairie
The treeless, grass-covered plains in the United States and Canada.

Predator
An animal that hunts, kills, and eats other animals in order to survive.

Rain forest
A forest with tall trees, a warm climate, and lots of rain.

Salt marsh
A marshy grassland area that is regularly flooded with salt water.

Sanctuary
A safe place.

Species
A group of living things that is capable of breeding together.

Stock
A supply of animals.

Swamp
An area of land that is usually waterlogged and overgrown.

Timber
Wood that is used for building or other commercial purposes.

Trait
A distinguishing quality that belongs to a person or animal and which can be passed down to their offspring.

Vaccine
A medicine used to treat illness.

Volcanic
Describes anything relating to volcanoes.

Further Information

Books

Animals at the Edge
Marilyn Baillie, Franklin Watts, 2010

Saving Wildlife series
Sonya Newland, Franklin Watts, 2010

Saving Wildlife (Action for the Environment)
Rufus Bellamy, Franklin Watts, 2006

Wildlife in Danger (Earth Watch)
Sally Morgan, Franklin Watts, 2005

Endangered Species (Saving our World)
Mike Unwin, Franklin Watts, 2003

Web Sites

www.worldwildlife.org
The World Wildlife site. Choose to sponsor an endangered species. You will see information and pictures of your chosen animal and learn how your gift will help protect it.

www.tusk.org
Tusk Trust funds habitat and wildlife conservation programs across Africa. Visit their web site to view the projects they support, and learn how you or your school could raise money to help their work.

www.wcs.org
The Wildlife Conservation Society is committed to saving the world's wild places and its wildlife. Learn about the threats facing bears, elephants, great apes, and many more endangered animals at this site.

Index

acid rain 22
agriculture 5, 12, 22
albino fish 27
alien species 5, 18, 19, 20, 21
American pikas 24
ammonites 4
amphibians 12, 14, 25, 29,
animal status 7
asteroids 4

bison 6
black rats 18
black robin 27
black-footed ferret 27
Borneo Orangutan Survival
  Foundation 17
butterflies 14

Californian condor 27
captive breeding 15, 26–27
carbon emissions 25
Christmas Island bats 23
CITES 10, 28
climate change 24–25
competition 18–19, 23
conservation programs 10,
  17, 28, 29
coral reefs 25, 29

deforestation 12
dinosaurs 4
diseases 23
dodo 20

early people 5, 6
ecotourism 29
elephants 8, 28, 29
extinction 4–5, 7, 20, 22, 24

ferrets 21
fish stocks 6, 7, 13
fishing 6, 7, 13, 29
flightless birds 20–21
flowers 23
fragmentation 14–15
fur trade 8, 19

giant pandas 15
global warming 24
gorillas 29
Great Barrier Reef 25, 29
Greenpeace 7
ground sloths 5

habitat loss 5, 12–13, 14–15,
  16, 23
hedgehogs 19
honey bees 23

inbreeding 14, 27
islands 5, 16, 18–19, 20, 21,
  23, 27
ivory 8, 10, 28

kakapos 21
kangaroos 18, 24
kiwis 21

leopards 9
Lewa Wildlife Conservancy 8,
  10–11

medicines 9, 10
moa 20

oceans 13
oil palm 16–17
orangutans 16–17
overhunting 5, 6–7, 20

palm oil 16
passenger pigeons 6
Père David's deer 26
pet trade 8, 17
poaching 8–9, 10, 11, 17
pollution 5, 22
possums 19
predation 18–19

rain forests 12, 16, 17
red squirrel 23
rhinoceros 10–11, 29

skins 9, 19
stoats 21
survival skills 27

temperatures 24–25
tigers 9
tortoises 5
tuna fish 6–7
turtles 13

Varroa mite 23

wetlands 12
whales 7, 29
white possums 24
wildlife parks 6, 10, 17, 29
wildlife stack 29
wombats 13, 24

Yangtze River dolphin 22
Yellowstone National Park 6